MASTERWORKS OF UKIYO-E

UTAMARO

by Muneshige Narazaki and Sadao Kikuchi

translation by John Bester

KODANSHA INTERNATIONAL LTD.
Tokyo, New York & San Francisco

Distributors:
UNITED STATES: Harper & Row, Publishers, Inc., 10 East 53rd Street, New York, New York 10022. SOUTH AMERICA: Harper & Row, International Department. CANADA: Fitzhenry & Whiteside Limited, 150 Lesmill Road, Don Mills, Ontario. MEXICO & CENTRAL AMERICA: HARLA S. A. de C. V., Apartado 30–546, Mexico 4, D.F. BRITISH COMMONWEALTH (excluding Canada & the Far East): Phaidon Press Ltd. Littlegate House, St. Ebbe's St., Oxford OXI ISQ. EUROPE: Boxerbooks Inc., Limmatstrasse 111, 8031 Zurich. AUSTRALIA & NEW ZEALAND: Book Wise (Australia) Pty., 104–8 Sussex Street, Sydney. THE FAR EAST: Toppan Company (S) Pte. Ltd. Box 22, Jurong Town Post Office, Jurong, Singapore 22.

Published by Kodansha International Ltd., 2–12–21 Otowa, Bunkyo-ku, Tokyo 112 and Kodansha International/USA, Ltd., 10 East 53rd Street, New York, New York 10022 and 44 Montgomery Street, San Francisco, California 94104. Copyright © 1969 by Kodansha International Ltd. All rights reserved. Printed in Japan.

LCC 68–26556
ISBN 0–87011–066–7
JBC 0371–780650–2361

First edition, 1969
Fifth printing, 1977

Contents

Translator's Preface 7

Utamaro 9

The Woman in Japanese Art 19

Japanese Titles of the Prints 30

The Plates 33

Translator's Preface

If art were merely a matter of colors, shapes, and textures, their organization and relationships, we should lose little in our appreciation of art of a different age and culture from our own. Even its alien themes, if intellectual comprehension were enough, would present no impossible barrier. But the part played in art by one further element—the emotional associations of familiar things—cannot be ignored. It is the intimate associations with our own past that, without our realizing it, set the mind scurrying around its private hoards of fear and joy, consolation and lust, drawing from them a complex and unconscious reaction that invests the work with its own unique atmosphere. This atmosphere is a perfectly valid element in the system of relationships that makes up a work of art, but it is the least universal, and does not export well.

This fact is particularly important in the case of much Japanese art and literature, which relies so heavily on references to the familiar. The Japanese, on the whole, refuse to see life as more than a sum of its parts, and are reluctant to make general statements or strike attitudes about it. On the other hand, they have a genius for isolating the familiar, trivial, or routine aspects of existence and by frequent presentation elevating them into easily recognizable symbols of what one might call the eternal values. The result is an art of association and suggestion, a kind of perpetual nudging of the mind.

This is not to suggest that Utamaro was trying, in his prints, to make any statement about "values." But it is true that they are full of hints and suggestions that to a cultivated Japanese will evoke a whole way of life. It is a way of life, moreover, that is not entirely dead even today, so that the associations for the Japanese are something more than a literary, theoretical nostalgia. The Westerner, conversely, loses a great deal if he makes no attempt to see any more in Utamaro's prints than patterns and colors and a remote, impersonal, abstract Oriental setting. The women Utamaro shows us may be idealized, but they are creatures of flesh and blood, who inhabit a very real world in which a great deal of human emotion is invested.

That world, in the sense of the physical environment, is a world of wooden buildings. Life in it is lived among soft textures of wood, paper, cloth, and woven straw. It is illuminated by daylight filtered through sliding screens, or by paper lanterns and candles; its smells are the smell of burning charcoal on a cold winter morning, of the steam from a wooden bath, of Japanese food. And the changes wrought in these familiar things by the seasons are recognized and organized into a well-known pattern that in itself gives life much of its meaning. To grow up in such an atmosphere is to develop a very different type of sensibility from one who has not.

It is, again, an exclusively feminine world—a world where women sit on their heels on tatami, viewing themselves in mirrors supported on lacquered stands; a world of kimono patterns, elaborate combs of wood and tortoiseshell, padded silken quilts, and perfume bags; a world of smothered laughter and the plaintive twanging of the samisen.

Most important of all, it is a world of gentle eroticism, of the unobtrusive yet pervasive eroticism that is one characteristic of Japan. At the heart of this world of Utamaro's—sheltered by wood, screened by paper, covered by the silks, barely hinted at yet inescapable—lies the contact of the flesh. In the all-feminine world of Utamaro's non-pornographic prints, all its grosser aspects are suppressed. Yet for someone familiar with Japanese life there are plenty of touches—a towel held by a woman fresh from the bath, a mosquito net, a summer kimono carelessly worn, an exposed nape of the neck, a posture—that, in sum, create an atmosphere as unmistakably sensual in its implications as many more explicitly erotic pictures.

Unfortunately, not only are the physical trappings of this Japanese sensuality unfamiliar to the West, but it also goes hand in hand with a different morality. Its relationship to the other areas of everyday life is as different from the corresponding relationship in the West as making love between quilts spread on the tatami is from making love on a bed. It follows that this exquisite world of faded colors and forgotten passions cannot stir the same nostalgic emotions in the Westerner as in the Japanese, and that an important catalyst in the process of artistic appreciation is lacking. Familiarity with Japan may help the foreigner to appreciate this side of Utamaro more, and even awake in him a kind of nostalgia for what he has never had. But for the foreigner who has never been there, an effort of the imagination is necessary if the work of Utamaro is ever to come alive for him in the same way as the art of his own culture.

J. B.

Utamaro

The worldwide fame that the name of Utamaro enjoys today contrasts oddly with his status in the society within which he lived and worked. In that society—on which feudalism imposed a formidable class consciousness—he was, quite simply, one of the common people who happened to earn his living by producing preliminary paintings for the popular woodblock prints. It is no wonder, therefore, that, as with many other ukiyo-e artists, we know very few details of his life.

Our basic source of information about him is a work known as *Ukiyo-e Ruikō*, a collection of notes on the lives and work of ukiyo-e artists, which is the starting point for research not only into Utamaro's life but also that of most other ukiyo-e artists. The section on Utamaro in the original version, which was published in Utamaro's lifetime, says:

> "Kitagawa Utamaro . . . [Details of his various pseudonymns, etc. follow.] At first a pupil of Toriyama Sekien, and studied the style of the Kanō school. Later did pictures of the gay quarters, lodging with Tsutaya Jūzaburō, the publisher of color prints. Did many color prints. Now resident in Benkei-bashi. Unrivaled in this age in the varied depiction of the gay quarters and beautiful women."

The *Meijin Kishin Roku* by Sekine Shisei (1825–93), a work second in importance only to the *Ukiyo-e Ruikō*, says:

> "Kitagawa Utamaro . . . a native of Kawagoe in the province of Musashi. Died at the age of fifty-three on the third of the fifth month, 1805. At first studied the style of the Kanō school, later became a pupil of Toriyama Sekien, establishing his own style and becoming a master of the ukiyo-e. Excelled at the portrayal of contemporary fashions and manners, and showed the polychrome print at its most brilliant. In 1804, did a picture of [the celebrated warrior and ruler of Japan] Toyotomi Hideyoshi and his five concubines, which was published as a color print on the sixteenth of the fifth month. It attracted official notice, and he was sentenced to three days in prison, followed by fifty days in hand chains. . . . At this time Utamaro was resident at Bakuro-chō."

Although this work puts the date of Utamaro's death at the third of the fifth month, 1805, records at the Senkō-ji Temple, where Utamaro's ashes were interred, state that he died at the age of fifty-three on the twentieth day of the ninth month, 1806. This record is almost certainly the more correct of the two, and it is by calculating back from the date it gives that the year of Utamaro's birth has come generally to be accepted as 1753.

The accounts also disagree as to the place of his birth. The *Meijin Kishin Roku*, as we have already seen, locates it at Kawagoe in Musashi. The *Mumei-ō Zuihitsu* says that he was born in Edo, while a work called *Ehon Tegoto no Hatsumei* says: "There was a painter called Roshō in Kyoto who went to the Kantō area in his middle years and took the name Kitagawa Utamaro." This has led some to conclude that he was born in Kyoto, but in fact all the existing theories seem to be little more than conjectures.

The one fairly definite clue we have is an entry dated the twenty-sixth day of the eighth month, 1790, that stands alongside an entry on Utamaro in the register (lost during the war) of the Senkō-ji Temple and records the death of a woman who was given the posthumous Buddhist name of Risei Shinnyo. There have been various theories about this woman, some identifying her with Utamaro's mother, some with his first wife, whose name seems to have been "Orio." Whatever her relationship to the artist, however, it is recorded that her ashes were interred at the Senkō-ji Temple only because her real family temple (i.e. where the whole family was registered) was too far away, the matter being arranged with the temple through the kindness of one Sasaya Gohei, a regular parishioner. This would seem to suggest that Utamaro himself was in fact born outside Edo.

He is believed to have been a pupil of Toriyama Sekien (1714–1788), since one of his works is signed "Utamaro, pupil of Reiryōdō," Reiryōdō being one of the pseudonymns used by Sekien, who was also known as Toyofusa. Again, in a preface to Utamaro's *Ehon Mushi Erabi* ("A Picture Book of Insects"), published in 1788, Sekien refers to Utamaro's childhood, telling how he had an eye for detail and loved to play with small creatures such as dragonflies and crickets. This indicates that Sekien knew Utamaro in his childhood, and makes it seem still more likely that he instructed him in the first rudiments of his art. Sekien, however, himself produced almost no ukiyo-e prints. A typical dilettante of the day, he had a passion for haiku and the type of humorous verse known as *kyōka*, and much of his work consists of *kyōka ehon*, illustrated books of humorous verse.

Utamaro also called himself "Kitagawa Toyoaki," as is witnessed by a signature that appears in the second of two illustrated volumes containing the libretto of a kabuki play, *Yonjūhatte Koi no Showake*, that was performed at the Nakamura-za theater at the New Year in 1775. Utamaro did the picture for the cover of this same libretto, the work being the earliest by Utamaro that has yet been discovered. It has usually been assumed that in using the pseudonymn "Toyoaki" Utamaro was following established practice and taking one-half of his teacher's name (Toyo-fusa). This theory is rejected by Kiyoshi Shibui, the well-known collector and authority on Utamaro, who considers that he devised the name himself, taking one character each from the names of two noted print artists, Ishikawa Toyonobu (1711–85) and Katsukawa Shunshō (1726–92), the "aki" of Toyoaki and the "shō" of Shunshō being written with the same Chinese character. As a picture of the actor Iwai Kumesaburō shows, Utamaro did in fact do actor-pictures in the Shunshō style, while Toyonobu was one of his predecessors in the field of pictures of beautiful women. However, this hardly seems to give grounds for assumptions about his artistic pseudonymn.

Following what—as far as we know—was his maiden venture, Utamaro did further work for the theater. In early 1778, and in the third month of the next year, he did the cover of a libretto for use at the Ichimura-za theater. In autumn 1776, he also did a print intended for distribution by the Ichimura-za in memory of Ichikawa Goryū (Ichikawa Goryū Nagori Sō-Yakusha Hokkushū), and in the eighth month of 1777, he did a picture book on the kabuki play Kanade-hon Chū-shingura, based on the celebrated story of the forty-seven rōnin (masterless samu-rai). All his known work of this period was for the theater. Later, when the threat of competition and a not unjustifiable pride in his art were to lead him to make rather boastful statements about his work, he was to claim that he never did actor-pictures, but in fact they were as indispensable a part of his apprenticeship as that of most other well-known ukiyo-e artists. It is interesting, incidentally, that pro-ducing pictures of celebrated prostitutes should have had more snob value than doing work for the theater.

Around 1779, with the publication of the sharebon Oki-Miyage, he began to do illustrations for the various types of popular literature current at the time. This literature embraced many types of work, including sharebon, yomihon, and kibyōshi, all of them popular novelettes on a wide range of subjects from the didactic to the erotic and always including illustrations. Other works of the same type from the same period include the yomihon Warabe-uta Kojitsu Ima-Monogatari, the hanashibon Susuharai, and the kibyōshi Tōto Kembutsuzaemon. Around his twenty-eighth year, he seems first to have started using the name Utamaro. Thus the kibyōshi Minari Daitsūjin Ryaku-engi has a preface by "Utamaro, dilettante of Sukiya-chō, Shino-bu-ga-oka." The colophon also has the inscription, "Pictures: Utamaro of Shi-nobu-ga-oka; Author: Enjū; Publisher: Tsutaya Jūzaburō," and a note by the author saying how he was tempted to consign the work to the wastepaper basket as unworthy of publication until persuaded to publish it by "Utamaro of Shinobu-ga-oka."

Thus we know for certain that Utamaro was living at this time at Shinobu-ga-oka—in the Ueno district of what is now Tokyo. The late Ichitarō Kondō linked this to the reference in the Ukiyo-e Ruikō to Utamaro lodging with the publisher

Tsutaya Jūzaburō, and concluded that he was living at this time with Tsutaya, who was then resident in Shinobu-ga-oka. Kiyoshi Shibui, on the other hand, believes that Utamaro was taken to Shinobu-ga-oka by Enjū, the author of the *kibyōshi* just mentioned, who found him in the more plebeian quarter of Ryōgoku, down by the Sumida River.

Whether Utamaro was actually living with Tsutaya or not, it is certain that the long and fruitful relationship between the two men began around this time. Hitherto, much of Utamaro's work had been done for Nishimura Yohachi, head of the house of Eijudō, which was currently publishing the work of Torii Kiyonaga. In 1780, two popular novelettes by Nishimura himself appeared with illustrations by Utamaro, but thereafter he seems to have broken with Eijudō and to have switched to Tsutaya, who, though a newcomer to print publishing, was a man of great ability. He was to publish not only Utamaro's best work but all the known work of Sharaku also, and it seems likely that the personal encouragement and assistance he gave Utamaro contributed greatly to his artistic development.

From around the time when he is believed to have started his acquaintance with Tsutaya, Utamaro began to produce prints, such as "Amidst the Flowers of Shinobu-ga-oka" and "Visiting the Gay Quarters Below Ueno," which depicted life in the unlicensed brothel district of the Ueno Hirokōji area. In 1788, his teacher Sekien died at the age of seventy-six, and in picture books published in the following year Utamaro indicated that he now considered himself to be artistically mature by using a signature which can be freely translated as "Utamaro, artist in his own right." From this time on, he began to abandon the type of work he had done hitherto—work for the theater, picture books, illustrations to popular novelettes, illustrations to books of humorous verse, pictures on historical subjects, pictures of ghosts—in favor of the pictures of beautiful women, which are the true province of the ukiyo-e. He produced a steady stream of such works in an ambitious new style of his own, and his idealized portraits of beautiful women soon won popular recognition under the name of "Utamaro beauties."

It is interesting at this point to consider what was happening in the world of ukiyo-e as a whole around this period. At the point in time when Utamaro can be supposed to have acquired a certain confidence in his medium and to have been ready to go on to his greatest achievements, the ukiyo-e had only recently entered the world of full color. It was in 1765, in fact, that the *nishiki-e*—the true polychrome woodblock print as opposed to the prints using a restricted number of colors that had been common before—first came into being. And in the rich colors and romantic idealism of the work of Suzuki Harunobu (1725–70), whose name is inseparably associated with the early *nishiki-e*, it attained at the very outset a high degree of artistic achievement. Harunobu's style inevitably had a great influence on the other artists of his time who did portraits of beautiful women, but following his death in 1770, they began to branch out stylistically along more independent lines of their own. The result was hardly a "reaction" to Harunobu's style, and the type of beauty portrayed was still highly idealized, yet it embodied a far greater element of realism than before.

Among the artists who produced this new type of *bijin-ga* ("pictures of beautiful women") were Kitao Shigemasa (1739–1820) and Torii Kiyonaga (1752–1815). Shigemasa, founder of the Kitao school, who was born fourteen years before Utamaro, was the son of a bookseller, but left the family business to his younger brother in order to become an artist. He produced a wide variety of works, including portraits of beautiful women, portraits of actors, "flower-and-bird" pictures, and landscapes. Possibly because he had private means, his total output was not great, but it includes not a single failure. Among the illustrations he did for *kibyōshi*, and in his picture books, there is also a great deal of first-rate work. His work has an unsentimental stylishness typical of Edo and a great technical distinction.

Torii Kiyonaga, born just one year earlier than Utamaro, was also the son of a bookseller. He studied with Torii Kiyomitsu, and did graceful brush paintings of beautiful women, which incorporated a strong realistic element. Also active around the same period was Utagawa Toyoharu (1735–1814), founder of the Utagawa school and, like Utamaro, a pupil of Sekien. During the An'ei and Temmei periods (1772–88), he was inspired by Western etchings and Western-style paintings to produce what were known as *uki-e*, prints showing scenes with an exaggerated Western-style perspective, which relied largely on their curiosity value. He also did richly colored, sensuous brush paintings of women.

Utamaro was to receive the direct and indirect influences of these older artists and to refine them in evolving his own style. Along with him, there were to appear a whole succession of other talented ukiyo-e artists, including the followers of the Kitao and Utagawa schools, Torii Kiyonaga, and Eishōsai Chōki, who studied under the same teacher as Utamaro. The period, in fact, is popularly known as the "golden age" of the ukiyo-e.

Following his emergence as an independent artist, Utamaro published a succession of polychrome diptychs of *ōban* (38.2 × 23 cm.) prints such as "Floral Charms for the Seasons' Amusements," and "Fashionable Amusements Amidst Fragrant Flowers" (Plates 1–3), and triptychs such as "Scene at Shichirigahama" and "The Picnic." In the use of two or three prints to make up a single work, Utamaro was clearly influenced by the compositional methods followed by Torii Kiyonaga in his full-length groups of women, and the coloring, too, is bright and cheerful in the Kiyonaga manner. The faces of his women similarly show the influence of other artists. Some works show the influence of Shigemasa, while in others the faces are taken almost directly from the works of Kiyonaga. Another interesting feature of some of these early works is the incorporation of *kyōka* (humorous verses). These suggest that Utamaro was on close terms with the authors of these *kyōka*, who formed a kind of literary elite within the merchant class of the time.

In these early works, thus, Utamaro drew freely on the styles of his predecessors in the effort to evolve his own style. It is only with works such as "By the Bridge at Ryōgoku" (Plates 4–5) that the type of idealized depiction of feminine beauty now associated with his name first put in its appearance. The same work is also significant for the way the color purple recurs throughout, giving a foretaste of the soft richness of coloring seen in his later works.

The qualities of Utamaro's art are still more in evidence in a series entitled "Geisha During the Niwaka Carnival in the Gay Quarters" (Plate 6), in which he shows geisha decked out in the costumes they wore for the annual Niwaka carnival of the Yoshiwara gay quarters. In the painstaking attention paid to the detail of the lavish costumes, one can still detect the influence of Kiyonaga and his emphasis on line, but the realism of the almost confusingly variegated colors (note that even the character for "painted by" in the three characters of the signature is printed in red instead of black) is quite typical of Utamaro. More important still, the work demonstrates the willowy treatment of the female figure that is so typical of the artist's best work.

Thus the characteristic features of the Utamaro style did not emerge all at once. Utamaro was, in fact, comparatively late in attaining artistic maturity. This is as true of his erotic works (*shunga*, "spring pictures") as of the rest of his output. As two authorities, Kiyoshi Shibui and Teruji Yoshida, have both pointed out, Utamaro, despite his popular reputation as a youthful eulogizer of a rather decadent type of feminine beauty, was already thirty-four when, in 1788, he produced the series of twelve *ōban* color prints known as "The Poem-Pillow Picture Book," perhaps the greatest of all erotic ukiyo-e. Kiyonaga, by comparison, was only twenty or so when he produced his first major erotic work, while Hokusai (1760–1849) is said to have done the illustrations for an erotic book at the age of twenty-three.

In 1790, just when Utamaro's fame was beginning to spread, the woman known posthumously as Risei Shinnyo died. The fact that in the two years that followed Utamaro produced no illustrated books at all has usually been taken as an indication of the grief this event caused him, even though his precise relationship to the woman is not known. It seems more likely, however, that the halt in the production of such books and the apparent absence, during the same period, of any prints showing full-length figures were both a result of his preoccupation with an entirely new type of print. This was the *ōkubi-e*, which showed only the head or upper half of the body.

Utamaro inaugurated the *ōkubi-e* in 1791, and it had an epoch-making significance in the development of his art. It inspired much of his best work, and for a while he seems to have abandoned all other forms. There would seem, for example, to be no full-length portraits corresponding to the period when Utamaro was producing ōkubi-e series such as "Ten Studies in Female Physiognomy" (Plates 10 and 13) or "Ten Feminine Facial Types" (Plates 11–12), which are characterized by backgrounds employing mica dust, and by faces which are rather fuller in the lower half. If stylistic similarities are any indication, his production of full-length figures would seem to have commenced again with the triptych "Needlework" (Plates 36–38), which uses a warm, cheerful yellow for the background and in which the faces have become somewhat narrower again. Such stylistic features would seem to place "Needlework" at around the same date as the later ōkubi-e series "Modern Beauties in Their Prime" (Plates 25–26) and "A Sundial of Maidens" (Plates 21–24), i.e. around 1792–3.

Many prints of Utamaro's early maturity portrayed courtesans in the Yoshiwara, the officially licensed gay quarters, thus fulfilling a public demand similar to the modern demand for pictures of movie stars. Now, however, he also did increasing numbers of pictures of women whose charms had brought them fame in the more plebeian roadside teahouses and in other similar places. In so doing, he obviated the troublesome routine required to gain access to the inmates of the recognized gay quarters such as the Yoshiwara, and was following an example set by Suzuki Harunobu, who had won great popularity with his portraits of similar women.

Like Harunobu, Utamaro set out to portray the popular teahouse idols of his time—women such as Okita of Naniwaya, Ohisa of Takashimaya, Toyohisa of Tomimoto, and Oseyo of Hiranoya. The first two of these in particular were the subject of many different pictures by Utamaro; they appear in many ōkubi-e and they also appear together in prints which show them engaged in various indoor pastimes symbolizing their rivalry for the public's affections. He even did works such as that shown in Plates 16–17, a technical tour de force showing the front and rear views of the same figure on reverse sides of the same sheet, which somehow gives credibility to the contemporary account of this particular beauty: "She had charm, and a beguiling tongue, and a civility in no way diminished by a niggardly gratuity. So great was her renown, indeed, that at times they were obliged to sprinkle water" (i.e. to start cleaning the premises, a sign that it was closing time).

There is a similar portrait of Ohisa, whose popularity was said to be a shade less great than that of Okita, and there are also—from a somewhat later period— prints which suggest a public curiosity about these idols' private lives no less edifying, perhaps, than that shown by today's cheap magazines. The portrayal of their faces, however, shows the idealization common to all Utamaro's work, and only the slightest difference in the line of the nose gives them any kind of individuality.

The same public curiosity about the domestic lives of their idols, applied in this case to the behind-the-scenes life of the gay quarters, gave rise to one of Utamaro's great masterpieces, "The Twelve Hours in the Gay Quarters," a series of twelve prints which depicts the daily round in the gay quarters from midnight until ten o'clock the following evening. Setting out to show what life was like behind the scenes, where the ordinary visitor to the gay quarters was not admitted, they provide many interesting contrasts. On the one hand, there is the weary, languid posture of the woman in "The Hour of the Ox" (Plate 48), trying to right an overturned slipper with her foot as she leaves the room to go to the toilet, or the relaxed, informal atmosphere of the women alone together in "The Hour of the Horse"; and, on the other hand, the professional expressions the same women show in "The Hour of the Monkey." Particularly skillful is "The Hour of the Boar," in which Utamaro succeeds in capturing the professional poise of a courtesan who remains cool and imperturbable in dealing with patrons at a saké party while her inexperienced young girl attendant is already nodding drowsily. Stylistically, the noteworthy thing about this set is the treatment of the female figures, which are impossibly tall and slender, with long, oval faces and delicate features. In these prints, one sees Utamaro's art at its most characteristic. They also, one might say, represent a high peak which he was never quite to attain again.

From around 1797, the sumptuary edicts that had been passed by the shogunate minister Matsudaira Sadanobu in an attempt to check the growing corruption and love of extravagance of Edo society seem at last to have begun to make themselves felt in restricting the technical extravagance of Utamaro's work—even though the author of the reforms had himself already fallen from power three years previously. Spiritually, too, the death in 1796 at the early age of forty-eight of Tsutaya Jūzaburō, the publisher who had done so much to put the best of Utamaro's work before the public, was undoubtedly a serious blow to the artist.

Utamaro had, in fact already been doing occasional work for an estimated total of more than forty publishers. Many of these works, however, were obviously tossed off rapidly, probably for the sake of the money, and are of very variable quality. Even granted that no artist could be expected to turn out an unbroken succession of masterpieces, it is remarkable how, in the period that followed Utamaro's attainment of full maturity, one finds prints of outstanding artistic quality rubbing shoulders with others of unquestionable mediocrity.

Among the more interesting works of this period are "Women Staying at an Inn" (Plates 41–43), "New Utamaro-style Brocade Patterns" (Plate 45), and "The Abalone Divers" (Plates 29–31), which exploit to the full the possibilities of woodblock techniques. Utamaro had always sought to give expression, not merely to superficial beauty of face or form, but to the inner beauty of the woman he portrayed. In these particular prints, however, he went further and experimented with various techniques, such as the omission of outlines or the use of red instead of black for the outlines, in order to suggest the soft textures of female flesh.

One cannot help suspecting that this attention to detail in the better of his prints of this period indicates not only an attempt to produce works of ever higher artistic quality but also an uneasy awareness of the inadequacies of his "pot-boilers" and their possible effect on his reputation.

During the Kansei era (1789–1800), Utamaro reigned supreme in the field of *bijin-ga*, yet even he was never able completely to ignore his rivals. This was particularly true in the cases of Hosoda (Chōbunsai) Eishi (1756–1829), who worked in the Kiyonaga tradition, and Hokusai (1760–1849), who, though still far from maturity, was enjoying a rapidly rising popularity.

Chōbunsai Eishi in particular had the advantage of being the eldest son of a descendant of the third lord of Tamba, who was also finance minister to the shogunate. He had studied painting, moreover, with Norinobu of the Kanō school, official painters to the Tokugawas. He entered the service of Shogun Ieharu, for whom he painted pictures, and enjoyed samurai status with a handsome yearly stipend. For some reason, however, he yielded his position as head of the family to his son, and went to study under an ukiyo-e artist called Bunryūsai who worked in the style of Kiyonaga, abandoning "classical" painting in favor of the ukiyo-e. His pictures of women—which show typical Kiyonaga-style tall, idealized beauties with much attention paid to the details of their costume—combine a willowy grace with a type of refinement uncommon in the ukiyo-e. He had a wide range of friends, spanning a broad section of society, and was surrounded by admirers who in their social status and tastes alike were rather different from those whom Utamaro could command.

That such a man should be sufficiently skilled as an artist to be ranked alongside Kiyonaga and Utamaro as one of the three masters of portraits of women must have irritated Utamaro, who had to work incessantly to make a living. This is apparent in the boasts that appear in some of his prints—on a letter held by a woman, for example, or in a special inset at the top of the print—which say "By the artist who depends on his own resources without imitating others," or, more frankly still, "Utamaro is unexcelled at pictures of beautiful women." Such overconfidence may well have been a sign of the dissatisfaction that is liable to set in after having attained the highest peak possible in one particular field. In fact, after "The Twelve Hours in the Gay Quarters," the postures of his women become increasingly stereotyped and insipid.

It seems that as a result of this Utamaro felt a need to give his themes more variety. The result was a series of full-length works dealing generally with the theme of motherly love—works such as "Seven Poetesses," "The Boy's Festival," and "Children Illustrating Well-known Sayings"—as well as pictures such as "Catching Fireflies," and "The Shower" (Plates 52–54), which were made up of three or five prints. Into all these works he obviously put his best, but they somehow lack the tautness and the artistic depth of his earlier masterpieces.

It was just when he seemed to be declining in his artistic powers that Utamaro suffered a blow that undoubtedly hastened his death. A book entitled "The Exploits of Toyotomi Hideyoshi," dealing with the life of the great general, had been enjoying an enormous vogue in Edo, and Utamaro, together with various other artists of the day, was tempted to trade on its popularity by producing prints on a similar theme. One result was the triptych known as "Hideyoshi Enjoying the Cherry Blossoms with His Five Concubines." Unfortunately, there was a government edict which specifically forbade the depiction of any famous warriors of periods later than the Tenshō era (1573–92), whether they were named explicitly or whether they were identifiable by other indications in the picture. Presumably because of this law, Utamaro incurred the shogunate's displeasure, and he was sentenced to three days in jail followed by fifty days in hand chains.

Following the incident, he was met by an even greater flood of orders for pictures. They may have been intended as a mark of sympathy by the publishers concerned, but they undoubtedly, by making him overwork, brought his death still closer.

Since this book is essentially a collection of reproductions of Utamaro's prints, the short account of his life given above has centered on this, the most important aspect of his work. However, not even the briefest account can be complete without some mention of his illustrations and paintings. As we have already seen, the artistic achievements of Utamaro's later years were based on a thorough apprenticeship in the art of illustration, undertaken before he ever turned to doing portraits of women. The *kibyōshi* and other works of popular literature which he illustrated at this early period are interesting for this reason, and also because, unlike single-sheet prints, they bear a definite date, which makes it possible for us to trace the development of his art. They suffer, however, from the crudity of the engraving. The work he did for the books of humorous verse, on the other hand, shows a far greater attention to detail both in the drawing and in the engraving, but it is impossible to appreciate them on the same artistic grounds as the prints.

A similar thing is also true, in some sense, of Utamaro's paintings of women. Admittedly, when compared with the prints, which were the result of collaboration between the artist and the men who engraved the blocks and did the printing, these works give us a more intimate idea of the skill of Utamaro's brushwork, and of his handling of color. They share, too, in that aura of uniqueness that any painting must have when compared with prints, of which many identical copies may exist. The fact remains, though, that for all the greater sense of closeness to the artist and the greater "realism" of a painting, it was the interaction of Utamaro's art with the restrictions imposed—and the possibilities offered—by the techniques of engraving and printing that gave his best work its peculiar distinction.

SADAO KIKUCHI

The Woman in Japanese Art

The ukiyo-e was a popular art created primarily by and for the common people of Edo during the seventeenth, eighteenth, and nineteenth centuries. To become truly popular, an art must take a form readily accessible to the masses; for pictures to become available to the public at large, they must be produced in great quantities. Thus the ukiyo-e included far more woodblock prints than paintings.

The ukiyo-e print as a medium capable of widespread dissemination evolved a characteristic organization of its own, a production and distribution system similar to the newspaper publishing business of today: the *hanmoto*, the man who ran the publishing business and provided the capital; artists, engravers and printers to work together at his bidding to produce the pictures; and a system of distribution by traveling salesmen or retailers. The one thing without which all this would have been impossible, however, was the society of the city of Edo, a city with a population already exceeding one million. The failure of the ukiyo-e to flourish on a similar scale in Kyoto and Osaka, the other two great cities of the day, doubt-less stemmed from the lack of factors essential for it to become a truly "commercial art"—chiefly, an enormous potential public.

As a popular art, the ukiyo-e had to be simple and straightforward in a way that would appeal to the common people, in this case the merchant and artisan class in a feudal society dominated by a samurai elite; not for it were the Zen-inspired profundity, the subtle appeal to the intellect. Its subject matter must be rooted in reality, appealing directly to the senses and the emotions, and it must have a readily appreciable relationship to everyday life if it was to find universal accept-ance. That woodblock prints should fulfill all these conditions says nothing, of course, about their artistic worth. Indeed, the need for the ukiyo-e to be cheap, and the fact that the values of Edo under feudal rule decreed that, in theory at least, the ukiyo-e was not worthy of the attention of "soldiers and gentlemen" had a gravely distorting effect on its value as art.

The subject matter was inevitably restricted. The public demanded, first of all, that the ukiyo-e provide a picture—preferably glamorized—of their own lives and the natural and man-made scenery of Edo and its environs. Its chief preoccupations, accordingly, were life in and scenes of the plebeian quarters of the city, especially the flat, low-lying areas bordering the Sumida River. Work after work depicts the changing seasons in Edo, the annual rituals of the Edo merchant class, and historic spots in and around the city.

Ukiyo-e prints were also required to serve as illustrated guides and as mementos for sightseers in Edo; it is no wonder that they were sometimes referred to as *Edo-e* ("Edo pictures") and considered to be one of the special products of Edo, suitable as souvenirs for people at home in other parts of the country.

The ukiyo-e, again, slavishly reflected shifting spheres of popular interest. Even the apparent widening of its range in the later stages of its development, when it took to depicting scenes outside Edo, was simply a sign that people were becoming conscious of those parts of the country that so far had lain beyond the narrow confines of their everyday experience. Ukiyo-e also reflected the Japanese public's taste for tales of olden times and its nostalgia for its own historical past; the number of ukiyo-e which, even if not dealing directly with historical subjects, show an awareness of history is very great. Yet another favorite theme of ukiyo-e were the various incidents and sensations that ruffled the surface of the society of the day. With little scope for movement or enterprise in a secluded country, a highly developed sense of history and an overdeveloped concern for the trivia of everyday life must have served to give at least some sense of variety and breadth to an otherwise restricted existence. It was for similar reasons that the other great group of themes of the ukiyo-e was provided by the amusements and entertainments of the merchant class—which, though unproductive if not downright immoral in the eyes of the feudal establishment, provided oases of light, color and pleasure in the dreary wastes of life under the Tokugawas.

These entertainments and amusements showed considerable variety, but the chief of them were three: sumo wrestling, the kabuki and popular music, and the gay quarters; and it is sumo wrestlers, actors, courtesans, and their surroundings that provide the ukiyo-e with its most constantly recurring themes. This is not to say that there were not many ukiyo-e that portrayed ordinary family life and the customs of the populace as a whole, but, as in the mass media of today, the focus was constantly on the popular idols of the time. The adulation accorded popular wrestlers, popular actors, popular prostitutes, and the more personable of the maidens who graced the unlicensed teahouses was every bit as ardent as that directed at their modern equivalents.

An important factor here, however, was that this society was a man's society—and a society, moreover, remarkably free from some of the inhibitions on sexual matters that, in the past at least, have dominated that of the West. It is no wonder, then, that of all the categories just mentioned it should be the women—and in particular the women of the gay quarters that played such an important part in the life of Edo—who provided the most popular subject of all. And it was Utamaro who brought this aspect of popular art to its highest peak.

Utamaro's pictures of beautiful women, and his half-length portraits in particular, were a special type of art that marked the beginning of a new phase in the history of Japanese art. Few artists can have shown such an exclusive preoccupation with women. Few artists can have probed so deeply into a world so universally feminine and yet so particular—a world intensely human and inhuman, equally remote from the ordinary business of everyday life and the austerity of the cloister, more remote still from the overtones of chivalry detectable in much of Western art. Yet Utamaro's women were not without their antecedents in Japan, whether in recent history or in ancient times, and it is enlightening to make a brief survey of changing ideals of feminine beauty as reflected in Japanese art throughout the ages.

The first examples of the portrayal of the woman in Japanese art (excluding *haniwa*, the earthenware figures found buried in or around early tombs) occurred in religious art, and are seen at their most characteristic in Buddhist sculpture. Good early examples are the "Kudara" Kannon at the Hōryū-ji Temple near Nara and the figures of Miroku Bosatsu at the Chūgū-ji Temple (fig. 1) near Nara and the Kōryū-ji Temple in Kyoto. With their almond eyes and their elongated faces with mysterious, timeless smiles, they were less portraits of the "feminine" than expressions in divine form of human aspirations, and those who gazed on them undoubtedly sensed a boundless compassion emanating from them.

This first, religious type of feminine beauty gradually merged into a second, more secular type. Somewhat later works, such as the figure of Kichijō-ten in the Yakushi-ji Temple and the Eleven-faced Kannon—said to be a likeness of the Empress Kōmyō—in the Hokke-ji Temple, represent a fusion of the human and the divine realized in terms of the aristocratic elegance of the Heian period. The Kichijō-ten, for example, though a religious subject, derives stylistically from the

2

same sources as the figurines of T'ang China and the "Lady Under a Tree" (fig. 2) in the Shōsōin Imperial Repository. With the figure of Amida Nyorai by Jōchō, in the Phoenix Hall of the Byōdōin Temple, the tendency is still more marked, the desire to inspire awe and reverence giving way to a desire to please pictorially. Eventually, with the Kamakura period and works such as the Benzaiten at Enoshima, on the coast near Tokyo, divinity is made subservient to femininity.

Statues of the native gods of Japan were probably

being produced as early as the first part of the Nara period (710–794), but those that survive from the later Nara and Heian periods (794–1185) —works such as the figures of the Empress Jingū and other female deities—show very few divine attributes to distinguish them from ordinary human beings, and convey an immediate sense of human presence. In this, they are in the same class  as the Enoshima Benzaiten (fig. 4); they are secular portraits of women, far from the faces of the continental-style Buddhas.

Where secular tastes in beauty were concerned, it seems clear from the "Lady Under a Tree" and the head of Kichijō-ten that the full-cheeked, well-rounded face—the same type of beauty that was fashionable in the Chinese capital of Ch'ang-an—was considered the ideal type of feminine beauty by the nobility of the Nara capital. This same type of facial beauty, now related to actual settings familiar to the aristocracy of the day, puts in its appearance in the *Yamato-e* of the late Heian period. Most typical of all are the beautiful court ladies to be seen in the celebrated *Tale of Genji Picture Scroll* (fig. 3). The high foreheads framed by long black hair, the thick, straight painted eyebrows, the eyes represented by single, horizontal lines, the thin hooked line that so modestly suggests the nose, the small, vermilion mouth and the plump cheeks seem to sum up the whole outlook of a leisured class.

In literature, a famous passage in the diary of the Lady Murasaki Shikibu, author of *The Tale of Genji*, makes a critical comparison of the physical appearance of a number of the ladies of the imperial court, and gives us a fairly clear idea of what was considered the ideal in feminine beauty at the time: delicate features, a fair complexion, plump, rather rounded cheeks, a well-formed nose neither too large nor too small, an expression of intelligence, a clear, untroubled brow, a charming expression of modesty concealing the slightest hint of a smile. Long, thin faces, angularity, large noses, anything too individual, were firmly rejected.

This type of face, the classical Japanese ideal, was to live on throughout the ages  in a whole style of *Yamato-e* painting which derived ultimately from the *Genji* scroll, and even in such aspects of the lives of the people as the dolls displayed in their houses at the Girl's Festival on the third day of the third month each year. It was obviously still alive, too, in the work of Sukenobu, Harunobu, Kiyonaga, and eventually, of Utamaro himself.

From the Kamakura period (1185–1333) on into the Muromachi period (1337–1573), the graphic arts, inspired by a new interest in realism, began to portray

a more individualistic type of face. The chief manifestation was the *nise-e* ("likeness"), which consciously set out to capture the inner spirit of the subject by faithful representation of the features. This new characteristic is apparent in a number of extant works, a celebrated example being Fujiwara Nobuzane's "Sanjūrokkasen" ("Thirty-six Celebrated Poets of Old"). It is doubtful whether the features of some of the women shown among the portraits of the thirty-six poets (not all of which are known to have survived) can really be called individual, but a few outstanding examples among the portraits of men suggest that there must surely have been some real individuals among the portraits of women poets that have been lost. This tendency toward the portrayal of actual human beings was possibly inspired by the portraits of Zen priests known as *chinzō*, which were presented by priests to their disciples as proof that they had transmitted the true teaching to them, and as such called for a high degree of realism.

The same kind of style is also apparent in the portraits of Yoritomo (fig. 5) and Shigefusa of the same period (twelfth century) and in the portraits of warriors that were popular in the fifteenth and sixteenth centuries, and clearly is carried on in such portraits of women as the famous late sixteenth-century painting of Maeda Kikuhime. Such realistic, individualistic portrayal is offset by the symbolic treatment seen in Nō masks (fig. 6) and puppet heads, which symbolize specific types of character rather than portraying actual individuals. There is a new, more plebeian type of picture, too, that typifies the new stirrings of life in the lower orders of society, and the new interest in humanity, in this early modern period. In the pictures of Okuni and other early exponents of the kabuki, of dancing girls, of married women with exposed breasts, of ill-favored, vulgar bathhouse prostitutes (fig. 7), there are signs of the age's new interest in human beings as such.

In this same period—around, say, the year 1600—Japanese history for the first time becomes the history of a single country, a country of sixty-odd provinces all on an equal basis; it is from now on that the ordinary people become the real driving force behind the national culture, as the early ukiyo-e so eloquently show. The pictures of women that, from some time around the 1660's, became the ideal of the common people were all inspired by actual human beings, selected in accordance with the changing tastes in female beauty of successive ages, and in this sense there was no looking back to the past. Even so, in the manner in which they are depicted they

seem almost to present—as though by some strange law of spiritual development—a kind of retrospective survey of the course followed by previous ages.

First, from Kambun (1661–1673) through Genroku (1688–1704) and on into Kyōhō (1716–36) times, the pictures of women include some in which prostitutes are treated almost as though they were figures of Buddhas or bodhisattvas. The women who appear in prints in the style of Kaigetsudō (fig. 9) are untroubled of countenance, healthy, plump, stylishly dressed, and very much in accordance with the taste of their times as we know it from, say, the writings of the novelist Ihara Saikaku. Yet their postures, with chin slightly drawn in, chignon protruding from the nape of the neck, shoulders back, belly thrust forward and skirt trailing on the ground behind, somehow call to mind such ancient Buddhist figures of the Asuka period as the "Kudara" Kannon (fig. 8). When they are shown with two girl attendants (kamuro), they recall the trinities of Buddha and two bodhisattvas common in Buddhist art.

The second phase extended from the Hōreki (1751–64) and Meiwa (1764–72) periods, when the chief exponents of the bijin-ga were Nishikawa Sukenobu in Kyoto and Suzuki Harunobu in Edo, on into the An'ei and Temmei eras (1772–81), when Torii Kiyonaga was the most famous figure. The two former artists seem to have been in thrall to the aesthetic ideals of the nobility of Heian times, and though their pictures of women were based on reality, something—possibly the artists' conscious infatuation with this art of the past—imbues them with an unworldly, dreamlike lyricism. The eyes and noses of their portraits are not, of course, the straight lines and delicate hooks of the figures in the Genji scroll. Indeed, the descriptions of beautiful court ladies given by Lady Murasaki Shikibu in The Tale of Genji suggest that the faces in the scroll—painted in the following century—represented a deliberate attempt to create a mood corresponding with that of the original novel rather than the contemporary taste in female features. In

the prints of Harunobu (fig. 10), the pupils of the eyes are clearly indicated. The modest, ladylike curve of the nose is flanked by delicate nostrils, and the tiny red lips, of the type seen in the Yamato-e, are given the faintest suspicion of a smile. Yet although the two eras are so different—although Harunobu's women are as often as not courtesans or common prostitutes—the figures depicted by Harunobu belong to the same world as those who inhabit the dreamlike depths of the Tale of Genji Picture Scroll.

It was Kiyonaga who awakened these plump, well-proportioned beauties from

their dream world and set them firmly in their own habitat on the banks of the Sumida River (fig. 11). Where, with Harunobu, the body was always somehow spiritualized, Kiyonaga sought his ideal type of beauty in an unequivocal union of the spirit and the flesh.

The third stage in the development of the bourgeois ideal of beauty was represented by men such as Maruyama Ōkyo and Tsukioka Settei in the Kyoto-Osaka area, and, in Edo, by the succession of artists from Katsukawa Shunshō to Kitagawa Utamaro and on to Chōbunsai Eishi and his school. With these artists, the sense of reality is heightened, and an effect of individual beauty is sought after in each of the women portrayed (not so much in the sense that the woman's face is truly distinctive in itself, as in the feeling the picture gives of being the portrait of an individual). To call this a return to the character depiction of medieval times as seen in the *nise-e* and *chinzō* would be carrying our parallel too far, yet the quality of the experience involved is, one feels, essentially the same. Indeed, there are clear signs that in the latter half of the eighteenth century, around the Temmei and Kansei eras (1781–1801), there occurred a new awakening to the existence of the individual in popular art. The interest in a new individualism based on a clear perception of the distinction between nature and man and between the self and others, which arose as a result of the new scientific and rationalistic outlook seeping into Japan from the West, played a major part both in Utamaro's portraits and in the art of Sharaku.

Our historical parallel ends here. For the period from the Bunka and Bunsei eras (1804–1830) until the end of the Tokugawa period in 1868, there is no equivalent in earlier times; it can be called, perhaps, the period of the degeneration of the Utamaro type of beauty. Out of the art of Utamaro's last years and that of the artists who followed him there gradually distilled a highly particular and highly localized view of what was desirable in a woman, a view that was summed up in the characteristically Edo concept of *iki*—a term which might be rendered as "stylishness" or "sophistication" but which, like all such terms, is really capable only of being experienced, not of being translated. The faces and postures of the women portrayed by Kunisada (fig. 12), Eisen, and other artists of the period are stereotyped symbols of this *iki*, and as such no longer recall the art of any previous age. They are sensual, sensational, over-sophisticated, artistically peripheral, worlds apart from the discreet, otherworldly creatures of the old *Yamato-e*. Their decadent gaze flickers from between half-open eyelids; their poses are oddly contorted; they have a strongly sensuous, almost reptilian quality. They mark the final decline of the culture of Edo, and the spiritual chaos that affected both men and women in the years preceding the fall of the Tokugawa regime and the beginning of the new Meiji era.

It is odd to think that in summing up the very essence of the Japanese ideal of womanhood—in creating women in whom one can detect characteristics of all those who preceded them in the long centuries of Japanese art—Utamaro should also, without knowing it, have been bidding farewell to that type and to the society that produced it. At the time of Utamaro's death, society was already slowly coming apart at the seams; and the "black ships" of the foreigners were less than fifty years away.

With the Westernization of Japan following the Meiji Restoration, a revolution in the appearance of the female has gradually undermined the traditional Japanese concept of feminine beauty. The underlying reason for this, of course, is the emancipation of women and their emergence as an influence on society at large. The type of beauty that Utamaro portrayed is no longer to be encountered on any casual stroll through the streets of what was the city of Edo. In certain very specialized areas of society, its outward trappings are preserved rather in the manner of an interesting cultural relic. But for the ordinary woman those trappings have become something very special, to be experienced just once in a lifetime when, at her wedding, she dons the traditional kimono and hairstyle of the bride. Even the aesthetic pleasure gained from the prints of, say, Utamaro, is for a Japanese inextricably mingled with a nostalgia for an age that can never come again.

What has been said of Utamaro so far may suggest that he was concerned solely to satisfy the requirements of a public that liked to look at pictures of pretty girls. This is a misjudgment, however, of both his depth and his range. As in the case of other ukiyo-e artists, Utamaro's *bijin-ga* center around female figures, and in many cases presuppose the existence of an actual woman who provided him with the model; in this sense, the whole of his work in this field can be described as the portrayal of attractive women. However, when one considers as a whole all the genre pictures by Utamaro in which such women are the central theme, it is apparent that Utamaro, again like other artists, was really treating them as one aspect of the life and manners of the city of Edo.

Viewed from this angle, his work is seen to range over a large number of subjects: the changing seasons and annual rituals—playing shuttlecock at the New Year, cherry-blossom viewing, summer evenings on the river, moon viewing,

firefly catching, saké parties in the snow, the five traditional festivals of the year—religious ceremonies, visits to the temples, theatergoing, visits to the gay quarters, trips to scenic spots, and so on. Women are shown at home, too—in the kitchen, doing needlework, spring cleaning—or engaged in various occupations peculiar to women, or even in carrying out such rural tasks as silkworm rearing. In other cases, the prints serve as miniature posters advertising various hairstyles or patterns for women's clothing as sold by the dry-goods stores. Very common, also, are prints showing a mother with her child, again in a whole variety of different poses and situations.

There are series of prints based on differences in women's dress according to class or occupation, ranging from the daughters of good families to merchants' concubines, prostitutes of various grades and even women divers on the seashore. Other series show women in a number of different poses associated with their daily activities—plucking their eyebrows, making up their faces, waking up in the morning, resting beneath a mosquito net, washing their hands, doing various kinds of manual work, and so on. Another of Utamaro's original ideas was the type of series portraying the activities of women at different hours of the day. One such series shows various types of women including a mother with her child, a maid, a daughter of good family, a kept woman, a shrine maiden, a teahouse girl, a merchant's wife, and a geisha, while others show a day in the life of the inmates of the Yoshiwara, who are seen preparing for bed, engaged in trivial chatter, after the bath, making up their faces, writing letters, at a saké party, in a palanquin, and in other scenes that arouse compassion before any other emotion, in the modern viewer at least. Utamaro's extraordinary creativity and curiosity led him to explore subjects that no one had touched on before. Quite obviously, his aim was not only to portray beauty of face and costume, but also to give a picture of one side of contemporary society and to probe into the world of women, and of female psychology, as they appeared to a man of sensibility.

When one examines the works which were intended specifically as *nigao-e*, i.e. facial likenesses, it becomes apparent that the "likeness" is not quite what we mean by the term today, nor even what it meant to some Japanese artists of the past. The pioneer in the portrait print of the Edo period was Katsukawa Shunshō (1726–92), who won fame with his prints portraying actors, and this particular type of *nigao-e* reached its zenith in the extreme realism of the art of Tōshūsai Sharaku, who was active in the years 1794–5. The work of the various *bijin-ga* artists also included many *nigao-e*, and for some time before Utamaro himself reached maturity the most popular courtesans of the day, as well as other young women famous for their charm, had been the subject of prints and of popular adulation. Utamaro's own work in this field represents a peak that no one else attained—especially in his great series of half-length portraits that began in the early 1790's. Yet even with Utamaro, there were obvious limitations to the extent to which the artist could stress individuality in the portrayal of beautiful women. In what was obviously a rather acid jibe at Sharaku's "excessive" realism, Utamaro once pointed out that in his own portrayals of famous lovers as they appeared in a kabuki play, he recognized that the actors played the roles precisely because they were handsome and beautiful respectively, and he was not interested in bringing out all the little idiosyncrasies of their appearance. The same kind of approach was clearly applied to his *bijin-ga*. In short, the *bijin-ga* as a genre in some ways resembled the beauty contest of today: individuality was a secondary consideration compared with beauty and regularity of feature.

The best years of Utamaro's life were devoted to the creative exploration of an idealized feminine beauty. However, around the turn of the century, in the 1790's and early 1800's, a change came over his work, and he began to show, as we have already seen, a new interest in the correspondence between human physiognomy and human character. He began to classify women's faces into a number of types— not all necessarily beautiful—and to apportion these types to different kinds of feminine temperament. This introduction of a theoretical, literary element undoubtedly marks a retrogression from a strictly artistic viewpoint, but in the early stages, at least, it resulted in some very fine work. One could cite a number of possible reasons for the change: a genuine interest in the inner psychology of women; a kind of artistic impasse created by Utamaro's refusal in later life to do anything, generally speaking, other than *bijin-ga*; the constant need to find something new to stimulate public interest; or the rather pathetic decadence of an aging artist committed to celebrating a way of life more suited to the young.

What of the women themselves? There is little need to dwell here on the restrictions that the feudal system imposed on the human beings who lived under it. Within that complex web of restraints, the courtesans who figure so largely in Utamaro's prints were bound still more tightly than the average citizen—bound by the personal beauty, the family poverty, or the other reasons that first led them to take up their profession. The superficial brilliance of their lives, the glamor that surrounded at least the more celebrated of them, must have concealed many a bitter personal tragedy. Cut off from their families, wasting away their lives under the anonymity of the fanciful names bestowed on them, they were forced to give themselves to a succession of would-be gallants, with little hope of being rescued from their surroundings by a rich man who would make them his mistress, and with no refuge in old age save the temple and the lonely grave.

There are restrictions, of course, even in a free society, and even these creatures who dragged out their existence in a cage within a cage doubtless managed, in their own way, to find some humanity. Yet their eyes, half-closed as though to keep any individuality safely shut up within, reveal that words such as freedom, human rights, and the like had not even entered the vocabulary of the society of the day. Edo ethics erected an insurmountable barrier between men and women. In the life of society, the two sexes existed at entirely different levels, and women were looked down on as vulgar and unspiritual, a view further encouraged by a religion that considered them to be creatures of sin and defilement. They were society's beasts of burden, the playthings of men, and the means of propagating the species.

It might seem strange that the most characteristic arts of the merchant class of Edo should have taken as their theme sex and romantic love, with women such as these as its focus. Yet it should be remembered that for the merchants of Edo "reality" was a world of restrictions, imposed on them from outside and essentially extraneous to their own personal feelings. The gay quarters that grew up in all the major cities afforded at least a negative kind of escape from that reality: from their own families, from their own society, even—for, as their art shows, they were constantly drawing parallels between themselves and the more glamorous past—from their own age. Thus it came about that, during their brief heyday, the great courtesans around whom that escapist world revolved lived like queens, in great mansions echoing the palaces of old, robed in costly garments, sought after by the rich and the famous of their society.

Their heyday past, most of them perished, but—by a strange irony—it is they, and not the men who used them in such lordly fashion, whose names and looks have come down to us today. The courtesan and the teahouse waitress live on in the art of Utamaro and his contemporaries.

MUNESHIGE NARAZAKI

Japanese Titles of the Prints

The titles of ukiyo-e prints often defy adequate translation, and the English versions given here are offered with diffidence as approximations intended mainly for the reader's convenience. Since they do not necessarily coincide with translations in other works on Utamaro in English, the original Japanese title remains the surest means of identifying a particular work. To help the reader who wishes to investigate further, the transliterated Japanese titles are appended in a separate list below. The figures refer to plate numbers. It should be noted that not all the prints bear original titles, and that some of the titles given are no more than descriptive labels attached to them by modern scholars.

1. Hagidera, from "Fūryū Hana no Ka Asobi"
2-3. Takanawa no Ki no Natsu, from "Fūryū Hana no Ka Asobi"
4-5. Ryōgoku-bashi Hashizume
6. Ōmando, from "Seirō Niwaka Onna Geisha no Bu"
7. Ga
8. Seirō Niwaka Onna Geisha no Bu
9. Sagi Musume, from "Tōsei Odoriko Zoroi"
10. Uwaki no Sō, from "Fujin Sōgaku Jittai"
11. Kemuri o Fuku Onna, from "Fujin Ninsō Jippin"
12. Fumi Yomu Onna, from "Fujin Ninsō Jippin"
13. Poppin Fuku Onna, from "Fujin Sōgaku Jittai"
14. Takashimaya Ohisa
15. Eri-yosoi
16-17. Naniwaya Okita
18. Matsubaya no Uchi Someyama
19. Yogoto ni Au Koi, from "Kasen Koi no Bu"
20. Fukaku Shinobu Koi, from "Kasen Koi no Bu"
21. Tatsu no Koku, from "Musume Hi-dokei"
22. Mi no Koku, from "Musume Hi-dokei"

23. Uma no Koku, from "Musume Hi-dokei"

24. I no Koku, from "Musume Hi-dokei"

25. Takigawa, from "Tōji Zensei Bijin Zoroi"

26. Hyōgoya no Uchi Hanazuma, from "Tōji Zensei Bijin Zoroi"

27–28. Odaidokoro Bijin

29–31. Awabi-tori

32. Kashi, from "Hokkoku Goshiki-zumi"

33. Teppō, from "Hokkoku Goshiki-zumi"

34. Tomimoto Toyohina, from "Kōmei Bijin Rokkasen"

35. Hinodeya Goke, from "Kōmei Bijin Rokkasen"

36–38. Hari-shigoto

39. Benitsuke

40. Keshō Ni-bijin

41–43. Fujin Tomari-kyaku no Zu

44. Gehin, from "Fūzoku Sandan Musume"

45. Fumi-yomi, from "Nishiki-ori Utamaro-gata Shin-moyō"

46. Ōgiya no Uchi Takigawa, from "Seirō Nana-Komachi"

47. Kamiyui, from "Fujin Tewaza Jūni Kō"

48. Ushi no Koku, from "Seirō Jūnitoki"

49. Tatsu no Koku, from "Seirō Jūnitoki"

50. Mi no Koku, from "Seirō Jūnitoki"

51. Inu no Koku, from "Seirō Jūnitoki"

52–54. Shūu

55. Yamauba to Kintarō: Chichi-fukumi

56. Yamauba to Kintarō: Kuri

57–62. Ryōgoku-bashi no Ueshita

63. Kanetsuke, from "Fujin Sōgaku Jittai"

64–66. Taikō Gosai Rakutō Yūkan no Zu

67. Momo no Kawamuki

68. Kameya Shiire no Ōgata-muki, from "Natsu-ishō Tōsei Bijin"

69. Namayoi, from "Kyōkun Oya no Mekagami"

70. Gūtarabei, from "Kyōkun Oya no Mekagami"

71. Bakuren, from "Kyōkun Oya no Mekagami"

76. Jūichi-danme, from "Kōmei Bijin Mitate Chūshingura"

1. *Hagidera Temple, from "Fashionable Amusements Amidst Fragrant Flowers"* ◆ *ōban* ◆ Tokyo National Museum ◆ This print is believed to have formed the right-hand half of a diptych. Despite its charm, there are evident signs of immaturity: the figures lack the flowing grace seen in later works; the lower half of the seated figure is weak; and the treatment of the fluttering sleeve of the figure in black is clumsy. All this, together with the square script of the signature, would seem to set the work's date in the early Temmei era (1781–89), around the time when the artist started using the name Utamaro. The grouping of the figures and their facial features betray the influence of Kitao Shigemasa.

2–3. *Summer in Takanawa, from "Fashionable Amusements Amidst Fragrant Flowers"* ◆ *ōban* diptych ◆ Tokyo National Museum ◆ The scene, a restaurant by the sea where a young man takes his ease with seven attractive women attendant on him, is typical of pleasure-loving Edo in the late eighteenth century. The square script of the signature, as well as the hairstyles and dress of the women, again suggest that the date of the work is sometime in the

early Temmei era. Perhaps through eagerness to establish clearly the nature of the setting, the artist has loaded the scene with rather too much detail—a fault he was to remedy in his later works. The contours of the faces show the influence of Kitao Shigemasa again, while the faithful depiction of the patterns of the kimono is doubtless an influence from Torii Kiyonaga (1752–1815), whose work was enjoying a great popularity at the time.

35

4-5. *By the Bridge at Ryōgoku* ◆ *ōban* diptych ◆ published by Tsutaya ◆ Tokyo National Museum ◆ The open space at one end of Ryōgoku Bridge was an amusement center for contemporary Edo. In these prints the bridge is shown very large, spreading out over both halves of the work to form a background that effectively sets off the six women who stand in the foreground—though the smaller figures in the background tend to detract from the boldness of the composition. The posture of the woman in the broad straw

hat faithfully echoes that of women in some of Kiyonaga's prints, and is a sign of how Utamaro was influenced by the other man who, though only one year older, achieved popularity earlier. The position of the legs of the central figure on the left suggests that the fluttering sleeve of the kimono is an attempt to suggest flowing movement rather than the effect of the wind. The predominant use of cool color gives the whole a restrained atmosphere characteristic of Utamaro's work.

青樓仁和嘉女藝者部

大万度

萩江
おいよ
竹次

哥麿画

6. *Ōmando, from "Geisha During the Niwaka Carnival in the Gay Quarters"* ◆ *ōban* ◆ published by Tsutaya ◆ Tokyo National Museum ◆ Geisha are said to have originated around 1762 when Kasen, a courtesan of the Yoshiwara, took to singing ballads with samisen accompaniment in the company of the male entertainers who were already popular at the time. In this print, one of a set of five, two geisha are seen donning special robes for a dance known as *ōmando* which was performed during the annual Niwaka carnival held in the gay quarters. Although the postures of both figures and the attention to details of their dress still recall Kiyonaga, the faces are already characteristic of Utamaro's own style.

7. *Painting* ◆ *ōban* ◆ published by Tsutaya ◆
British Museum, London ◆ This print was
probably one of a set illustrating the "four
elegant pastimes." The official seal in the
circle above the vine-leaf trademark of
the publisher suggests that the print was
produced after 1790, when the system of
inspecting prints before publication was inaugurated. The handsome young man surrounded by beauties was perhaps intended to
represent Utamaro himself. The unusual
composition, with the figures clustered on the
right-hand side of the print, shows that
Utamaro's style was coming into its own.

8. *Geisha During the Niwaka Carnival of the Gay Quarters* ◆ *ōban* ◆ published by Tsuruya ◆ private collection ◆ Utamaro's earlier series on the same theme (see Plate 6) still betrays the influence of Kiyonaga, but this print, which is typical of his style during the Kansei era (1789-1801), shows that style close to full maturity. Technically, the print is more lavish, and uses a mica-dust background. The figures are labeled according to the roles they portrayed in the carnival, but they were doubtless recognized by Utamaro's contemporaries as representations of celebrated geisha of the day.

40

9. *Heron Maiden, from "A Set of Contemporary Dancers"* ◆ *ōban* ◆ published by Tsutaya ◆ private collection ◆ This is one of a series of prints that shows girls performing dances based on various popular legends. Such themes were favorites of ukiyo-e artists, but Utamaro was the first to concentrate on the faces rather than the figures of the dancers. The work, which is believed to date from somewhat before the Kansei era (1789–1801), retains a certain fresh, naive quality while hinting at the full maturity of the artist that was only a few years away.

11. *Woman Smoking, from "Ten Feminine Facial Types"* ◆ *ōban* ◆ published by Tsutaya ◆ Tokyo National Museum ◆ This series pre-ceded that shown in Plate 10. The "no-non-sense" air of the woman suggests that she was, perhaps, a teahouse girl.

10. *The Flirt, from "Ten Studies in Female Physiognomy"* ◆ *ōban* ◆ published by Tsutaya ◆ Important Cultural Property ◆ Tokyo National Museum ◆ This work is one of the finest of all Utamaro's "character studies" of women.

12. *Woman Reading a Letter, from "Ten Feminine Facial Types"* ◆ *ōban* ◆ published by Tsutaya ◆ Kiyoo Yamamoto collection ◆ This print, which bears only the title of the series, is notable for skillfully catching the concentration with which the woman is reading her letter, holding it up to the light in order to see better.

婦人相學十躰

相見　歌麿画　

13. *Woman Playing a Poppin, from "Ten Studies in Female Physiognomy"* ❖ *ōban* ❖ published by Tsutaya ❖ Honolulu Academy of Art ❖ This print was originally included in the "Ten Feminine Facial Types" series.

The *poppin* was a kind of musical toy that enjoyed a vogue around the Kansei era. The woman has an air of relaxed self-assurance that suggests she is the daughter of, say, some wealthy merchant family.

14. *Ohisa of Takashimaya* ◆ *ōban* ◆ published by Tsutaya ◆ Seiichirō Takahashi collection ◆ Ohisa of the teahouse Takashimaya was one of the most celebrated beauties of her day, and, along with Okita of Naniwaya, was one of Utamaro's favorite subjects.

15. *Powdering the Neck* ◆ *ōban* ◆ published by Isemago ◆ private collection ◆ The nape of the neck is considered especially attractive, while there is also a suggestion—with certain erotic overtones—that the woman has just come from the bath.

46

16–17. *Okita of Naniwaya (obverse and reverse)* ◆ *hosoban* (33 × 14.3cm.) ◆ private collection ◆ Okita was reputedly a girl of unfailing charm and good temper. Utamaro was fond of portraying both her and Ohisa of Takashimaya (Plate 14). This work stands out as a technical tour de force since it shows the subject from both the front and the rear, on opposite sides of the same sheet of paper, the outlines of the two figures corresponding almost exactly. The effect is to provide an extraordinarily lifelike image of Okita, demurely advancing to attend to a customer, with a cup of tea in one hand and a tray of smoking utensils in the other.

48

松葉屋内
深山
そみじ
そ生の

歌麿筆

18. *Someyama of Matsubaya* ◆ *ōban* ◆ published by Murataya ◆ Susumu Uchiyama collection ◆ Someyama's voluminous outer garment, with its brilliant floral pattern, seems to be vying with the cherry blossoms overhead. She was a celebrated courtesan, but it is in her dress rather than her facial features that the interest of the print lies. The doll borne by one of the courtesan's attendants is holding a *poppin*, a type of musical toy that was all the rage among the women of contemporary Edo. The Yoshiwara was a source of passing fashions, while the ukiyo-e, like the popular magazines of today, reflected these fads.

49

19. *Love Meeting Nightly, from "Selected Poems: On Love"* ✦ *ōban* ✦ published by Tsutaya ✦ Tokyo National Museum ✦ Other known plates from this series include the jacket illustration and "Love Brooding" (Plate 20), and two others. Like "A Set of Contemporary Dancers" (Plate 9), they have the youthful freshness and the mica-dust backgrounds typical of Utamaro's work in the period immediately preceding its fullest maturity. The title of this particular print was not known until a copy bearing it came up for auction in London a few years ago.

20. *Love Brooding, from "Selected Poems: On Love"* ◆ *ōban* ◆ published by Tsutaya ◆ private collection ◆ The woman in this print is caught in a private, pensive mood. She holds a slender pipe in her hand and expels smoke with an almost audible sigh, her parted lips revealing a glimpse of black-enameled teeth as she does so.

21. *The Hour of the Dragon, from "A Sundial of Maidens"* ❖ *ōban* ❖ published by Murataya ❖ Important Cultural Property ❖ Tokyo National Museum ❖ This and the next three prints are all from the same series, showing young women of the merchant class at various hours from morning until afternoon. In this work, the two girls have just risen and washed.

22. *The Hour of the Snake, from "A Sundial of Maidens"* ❖ *ōban* ❖ published by Murataya ❖ Important Cultural Property ❖ Tokyo National Museum.

52

娘日時計　午ノ刻

古代者女湯以甲刻
當当此圖﹅

哥〱麿筆

23. *The Hour of the Horse, from "A Sundial of Maidens"* ◆ *ōban* ◆ published by Murataya ◆ Important Cultural Property ◆ Tokyo National Museum ◆ These two beauties have obviously just emerged from the bath. One is still drying her ears, while the other is wringing out her towel, holding a bag of rice bran (used for washing at that time) between her teeth. Two further characteristics of the series are the yellow backgrounds and the great attention paid to the tasteful combination of colors in the clothing.

娘日時計申ノ刻

24. *The Hour of the Boar, from "A Sundial of Maidens"* ✦ *ōban* ✦ published by Murataya ✦ Important Cultural Property ✦ Tokyo National Museum ✦ It is four in the afternoon, and at last we see a young woman sallying forth in her finery—to the theater, perhaps? —with another young woman in attendance. She is so attentive to the set of her collar that she seems not to have noticed that her obi is slipping.

25. *Takigawa, from "Modern Beauties in Their Prime"* ◆ *ōban* ◆ published by Wakasaya ◆ Tokyo National Museum ◆ This series comprises some twelve prints in all, but incorporates all four of a previously published set of prints entitled "Portraits of Beauties in Their Prime," which is believed to date from 1794. In this print, the courtesan Takigawa is shown with head bent forward, absorbed in the letter clutched almost secretively in her hands.

56

26. *Hanazuma of Hyōgoya, from "Modern Beauties in Their Prime"* ◈ *ōban* ◈ published by Wakasaya ◈ Tokyo National Museum ◈ Utamaro may have objected to the "excessive" realism of Sharaku, yet even in essentially non-individualistic portrayals of famous beauties there is—quite apart from the variety of composition achieved within such a restricted theme—a considerable variety of feeling in the facial expressions. In the depiction of this young woman as she turns round, screwing up a letter in her hand, there is a suggestion of some strong, suppressed emotion.

27-28. *Beauties in the Kitchen* ◆ *ōban* diptych ◆ published by Uemuraya ◆ Tokyo National Museum ◆ This work is a good example
of Utamaro's skill in capturing women in every possible pose, even
those associated with humdrum activities such as cooking, washing
their hair, needlework, applying cosmetics and so on. Each of the

women shown here—the mother whose child is clinging to her as she wipes a dish, the woman peeling a persimmon, the woman blowing on the fire through a bamboo tube, the woman involuntarily screwing up her face because of the steam as she ladles out some boiling water—has her own characteristic pose and expression.

29-31. *The Abalone Divers* ❖ *ōban* triptych ❖ Susumu Uchiyama collection ❖ Although women divers were a comparatively common theme for the ukiyo-e, no other work achieved the artistic excellence of this, one of Utamaro's most celebrated works. Very few complete copies survive. Utamaro tried various means of

conveying the texture of female flesh, sometimes, as in "A Sundial of Maidens" (Plates 21-24), omitting the outline of the face, sometimes relying on the texture of the paper used and the contrast with the color of the background. In this work, he makes most effective use of flesh-colored outlines for the faces and bodies.

32. *Kashi, from "Five Shades of Black in the Yoshiwara"* ❖ *ōban* ❖ published by Isemago ❖ Kinosuke Hirose collection ❖ The name of this series obviously refers to the five grades of low-class prostitutes and entertainers in the Yoshiwara—a subject that allowed Utamaro to probe beyond the brilliant exterior and portray human nature with a new insight.

33. *Teppō, from "Five Shades of Black in the Yoshiwara"* ❖ *ōban* ❖ published by Isemago ❖ private collection ❖ This work is a masterly portrayal of wanton sensuality.

62

34. *Toyohina of Tomimoto, from "Six Celebrated Teahouse Beauties"* ◈ *ōban* ◈ published by Ōmiya ◈ Seiichirō Takahashi collection ◈ Some of the prints in this series reappear, with some alterations, in another series entitled "Six Poets of Fashion." Both are believed to date from sometime around the mid-1790's. The small pictures in the inserts symbolize the names of the respective teahouses.

35. *Widow at the Hinodeya, from "Six Cele-brated Teahouse Beauties"* ◆ *ōban* ◆ published by Ōmiya ◆ Seiichirō Takahashi collection ◆ This woman has shaved her eyebrows—a sign of the older woman—and one wonders if she was forced to work at the teahouse because of reduced circumstances. Her charm is different from that of the younger women shown in some other prints. The same woman, with eyebrows added, appears again in another series.

36–38. *Needlework* ◆ *ōban* triptych ◆ published by
Uemuraya ◆ British Museum, London ◆ The relaxed,
happy atmosphere of this scene is enhanced by the warm
yellow background against which the graceful figures
stand out as in relief. An interesting feature of the work
is the new attempt to give the composition depth by

placing the child and cat on the right in front of the three main figures and the central figure of the woman with an insect cage behind them. This type of composition also serves to increase the feeling of distance between the two women, one older, one younger, who are shown measuring a piece of cloth. The simplifica-tion of line and the reduction in the number of colors used—two characteristics shared with the ōkubi-e series—are typical of Utamaro's mature style. The figure of the young mother on the left has a great sense of repose and gentleness, and the veil-like effect of the gauze she holds is a touch of great beauty.

67

39. *Applying Lip Color* ❖ *ōban* ❖ published by Uemuraya ❖ British Museum, London ❖ The woman here has blackened her teeth with enamel, and is now applying color to her lips.

Utamaro captures her expression with extraordinary skill. Note the bold lines of the clothing in comparison with the delicacy of the face.

40. *Two Beauties at Their Toilet* ❖ *ōban* ❖ published by Uemuraya ❖ private collection ❖ Particularly beautiful here are the curves formed by the pose of the woman in the foreground.

婦人泊り客之圖 三枚續

41–43. *Women Staying at an Inn* ❧ *ōban* triptych ❧ published by Tsuruya ❧ Kiyoo Yamamoto collection ❧ The composition of this celebrated work—with the mosquito net spreading across all three prints and its six women, three seated inside and three standing outside the net—is unlike anything seen in the earlier triptychs. Utamaro's consummate skill is apparent in the way he places his women on both sides of the net in order to create a sense of depth,

and also in the sense of stability achieved through the variation in
their heights. What was probably of still greater interest to the
artist, however, was the effect of the yellow background and the
green net in enhancing the grace of the figures, and the subtle
variations in color between the women inside the net and those
outside. The fine mesh of the net was achieved by the use of two
blocks, one for the vertical lines and one for the horizontal.

44. *The Lower Grade, from "Three Grades of Maidenly Manners"* ◆ *ōban* ◆ published by Wakasaya ◆ Tokyo National Museum ◆ This is one of a set of three prints, each showing one seated and one standing figure against a yellow background. The idea of depicting young women from three different classes of society enabled Utamaro to exercise his characteristic sensitivity to color, the comparatively bright, unconsidered color combinations seen in the clothing of this print giving way in "The Upper Grade" print to subtler, more sober hues. However, the faces all have typically idealized features.

45. *Reading a Letter, from "New Utamaro-style Brocade Patterns"* ✦ *ōban* ✦ published by Tsuruya ✦ Susumu Uchiyama collection ✦ This print clearly shows how Utamaro dispensed with unnecessary line and relied on areas of color. In this series, he used a combination of techniques already applied successfully in other works—vermilion line for the face, black line for the hands, and no line for the clothing, together with embossing and other refinements of the woodblock print. Utamaro was obviously proud of this series; the text at the upper left of the print is a scathing attack on other artists' crude use of color.

46. *Takigawa of the Ōgiya, from "The Seven Komachi of the Gay Quarters"* ◆ ōban ◆ published by Izumisa ◆ Seiichirō Takahashi collection ◆ "Seven Komachi" occurs frequently in the titles of ukiyo-e works. "Komachi" refers to Ono no Komachi, the celebrated Heian era poet, while "Seven" refers to seven well-known episodes associated with her. The ukiyo-e series is intended to provide "latter-day versions" of these episodes, but the connections are often tenuous, while sometimes, as here, the title is the merest pretext for a series of seven works. The signature—"the genuine Utamaro"— indicates how Utamaro's mounting fame had increased the number of his imitators.

74

婦人白業拾二工

47. *Hairdressing, from "Ten Typical Feminine Skills"* ◆ *ōban* ◆ published by Wakasaya ◆ private collection ◆ All twelve prints of this series, which dates from around the Kyōwa era (1801–3), are extant. Each shows two figures, sometimes two women and sometimes one woman and one man. The faces of the women have little individuality, and the series is a collection of typical "Utamaro beauties."

75

48. *The Hour of the Ox, from "The Twelve Hours in the Gay Quarters"* ◆ *ōban* ◆ published by Tsutaya ◆ Seiichirō Takahashi collection ◆ This and the following three prints all depict scenes in the gay quarters of the Yoshiwara from midnight until ten in the evening (the day was divided up into twelve periods corresponding to two modern "hours," the first lasting from 11:00 P.M. to 1:00 A.M. and the last from 9:00 to 11:00 P.M.). The women in this series, like the one shown in this print, are mostly shown, not in their finery with elaborate hairstyles, but in more relaxed garb and postures. The hour of the ox is the period from one to three in the morning.

49. *The Hour of the Dragon, from "The Twelve Hours in the Gay Quarters"* ◆ *ōban* ◆ published by Tsutaya ◆ Seiichirō Takahashi collection ◆ The placing of the two figures at different heights in this charming scene, and the bold way in which a large space is left blank, are typical features of the prints in this series. The time is between seven and nine in the morning, and the women would appear to be going to bed. However, it is doubtful whether the times are to be taken literally; it seems more likely that the titles are merely a convenient framework for a set of twelve varied scenes.

50. *The Hour of the Snake, from "The Twelve Hours in the Gay Quarters"* ◆ ōban ◆ published by Tsutaya ◆ Seiichirō Takahashi collection ◆ The standing woman appears to have just emerged from the bath, and the young attendant has brought her a cup of tea. The elongation of the female figure that characterizes Utamaro's prints reached its most extreme form in this series, coinciding with the extreme delicacy of form, color, and feeling that sets it at the artistic peak of his entire career.

78

51. *The Hour of the Dog, from "The Twelve Hours in the Gay Quarters"* ◆ ōban ◆ published by Tsutaya ◆ Seiichirō Takahashi collection ◆ A courtesan turns from the letter she is writing to whisper something to her young attendant. The great courtesans had two of these attendants, known as *kamuro*; they were destined in time to become prostitutes themselves, though few would attain the same heights as their erstwhile mistresses. The men who frequented the gay quarters —as in most Utamaro prints apart from his erotic works—are conspicuous by their absence.

52–54. *The Shower* ◆ *ōban* triptych ◆ published by Tsuruya ◆
private collection ◆ The sudden shower, with the opportunity it
provided for showing people running, putting up umbrellas, and
seeking shelter under trees, was a favorite theme for ukiyo-e artists.
In this triptych, people from various walks of life are shown taking

shelter under a single large tree. Compared with earlier triptychs, particularly those of the Temmei era, the handling of the large area of three sheets shows considerably greater skill, but the sense of movement that is apparent in each individual print loses much of its effect when the work is seen as a whole.

55. *Yamauba and Kintarō: Kintarō at the Breast* ◆ *ōban* ◆ published by Tsutaya ◆ Tokyo National Museum ◆ Around the Kyōwa era (1801–1804), Utamaro did some thirty prints on the theme of Kintarō, an infant of prodigious strength and ruddy complexion. According to legend, Kintarō was brought up by his mother, Yamauba ("Mountain Mother") in the forest, and grew up to be a great hero. This print, a good example of its kind, skillfully captures the beauty and wildness of Yamauba, the mischievousness in Kintarō's eyes, and the trust and affection that bind mother and child.

56. *Yamauba and Kintarō: The Chestnuts* ◆ *nagae-ban* (67 ×
15.8cm.) ◆ published by Murataya ◆ private collection ◆ Many
reasons have been suggested for the sudden spate of Yamauba-
Kintarō prints, but a major one was probably, quite simply, the
appeal of the "motherly love" theme for Utamaro's public.
Skillful advantage is taken of the *nagae-ban* shape in the composition. Much credit must go to the unknown engraver for the
quality of his work, especially with Yamauba's hair.

57-62. *On and Below Ryōgoku Bridge* ◆ six ōban prints ◆ published by Ōmiya ◆ Tokyo National Museum ◆ This work is unusually large for the ukiyo-e. Equally unusual is the large number of figures shown—thirteen above and ten below the bridge. The women, tall with elongated faces, are typical "Utamaro beauties." The composition, with the bridge spreading boldly across all six prints, is interesting, and Utamaro has succeeded in creating six related prints that are also compositionally satisfying when viewed singly. The faces, though stylized, manage to convey individual differences of temperament. The color is gay, and the whole work has a brilliance and life that vividly suggest a summer's day in old Edo —even if that ideal city only existed in the artist's own imagination.

84

婦人相學拾躰

此れ玉ての懐やらく
〆く万すふ〱〱
ましらてっ〱
わらさこ
〱るり

觀相歌麿

63. *Blacking the Teeth, from "Ten Studies in Female Physiognomy"* ◆ *ōban* published jointly by Tsuruya and Yamashiroya ◆ Seiichirō Takahashi collection ◆ Another series, also entitled "Ten Studies in Female Physiognomy," was published by Tsutaya Jūzaburō. The print shown here, however, belongs to a group with the same title that was published jointly by Tsuruya and Yamashiroya. Produced sometime in the Kyōwa era, the group shows faces that have the harder, stereotyped quality that characterizes Utamaro's last work, individuality being suggested less by the face than by details of dress and the general posture.

64–66. *Hideyoshi Enjoying the Cherry Blossoms with his Five Concubines* ◈ *ōban* triptych ◈ Shigeyuki Nomura collection ◈ This is the work that brought Utamaro into disfavor with the shogunate. The triptych ignored an edict designed to stifle criticism of the Tokugawa family's ancestors, and its publication resulted in Utamaro's being sentenced to three days in jail and fifty days in hand chains. The

prints were inspired by a *yomihon* entitled "The Exploits of Toyotomi Hideyoshi," that was published in a number of volumes sometime between 1797 and 1802. The scene portrays the famous cherry–blossom viewing party that Hideyoshi held in 1598 at Daigo in Kyoto.

67. *Peeling a Peach* ◆ *ōban* ◆ published by Yamaguchiya ◆ Seiichirō Takahashi collection ◆ With her sleeves rolled up in business-like fashion, a young woman peels a peach while the child at her knee watches expect- antly. The children in ukiyo-e prints fre- quently appear very old, but here the child's intense expression, contrasting with the mild look on the woman's face, conveys something that is essentially childlike.

88

68. *Kimono for the Larger Woman, at the Kameya Store, from "Contemporary Beauties in Summer Garb"* ◈ *ōban* ◈ Tokyo National Museum ◈ A tall, amply proportioned woman is shown dressed in a bold-patterned kimono that creates a clean-cut, unpretentious effect typical of the taste of contemporary Edo. The title suggests that these prints were intended, not for sale in the usual way, but as advertisements for new fashions being put on sale by the leading dry goods stores of the day.

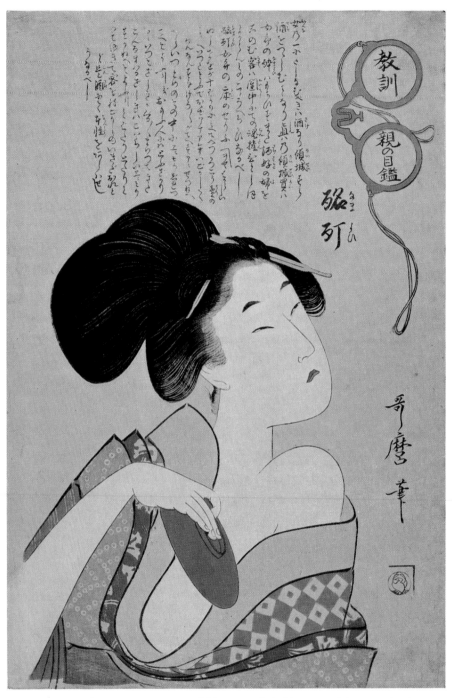

69. *The Tippler, from "Warnings to Watchful Parents"* ◆ *ōban* ◆ published by Tsuruya Seiichirō Takahashi collection ◆ This series, which consists of ten prints, is one of the better works produced by Utamaro during the first few years of the nineteenth century. The various undesirable types of character that he sets out to portray are conveyed quite effectively, though one cannot help sensing a decline in the artist's powers. Each print carries a short text describing, in somewhat moralizing terms, the character portrayed.

90

70. *The Half-baked Type, from "Warnings to Watchful Parents"* ◆ ōban ◆ published by Tsuruya ◆ Seiichirō Takahashi collection ◆ The woman shown here is cleaning her teeth and has her mouth full of water, which she is leaning forward to spit out. The text describes her as "never known to go against another's advice, nor to make an effort on her own initiative; she is not particularly delighted by the pleasant, nor put out by the depressing . . she does neither harm nor good . ." And it adds a little homily on the responsibility of the parent in forming the child's character.

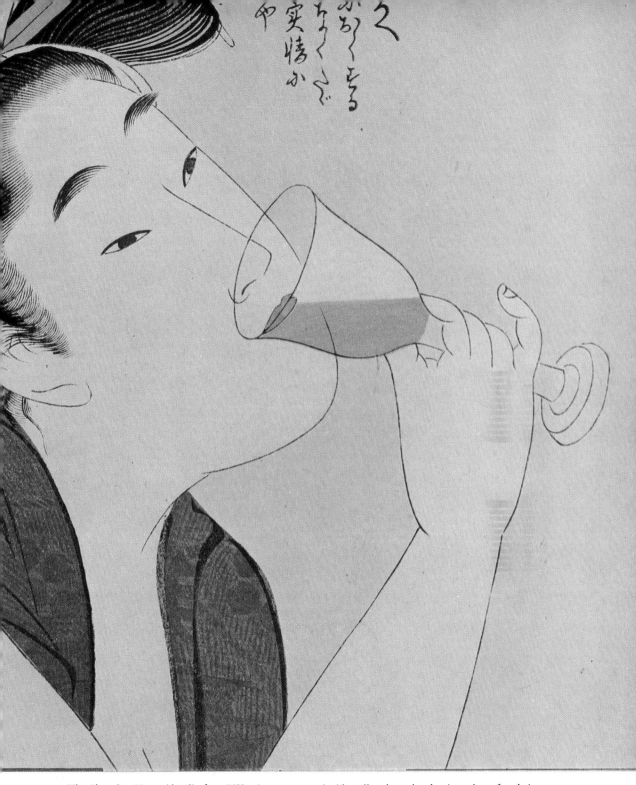

久
かぶくも
ちくくで
実情か
や

71. *The Shameless Hussy (detail), from "Warnings to Watchful Parents"* ◆ ōban ◆ published by Tsuruya ◆ Seiichirō Takahashi collection ◆ This young woman, according to the text, prides herself on not worrying about appearances. She does what she wants to, without troubling about what people will think— nor, incidentally, does she despise others for their faults. She is not willing to learn from others, and her insistence on behaving "naturally" means that her faults are plain for all to see. . . . The glass she is drinking from with such apparent enjoyment would have been something of a rarity in Utamaro's day.

93

72-75. The plates on this and the following page are examples from the Seiichirō Takahashi collection of illustrations for the books of humorous verse known as *kyōka-ehon*. The titles are, on this page, *Fugen-zō* (above and below) and on the facing page, *Gin-Sekai* (above) and *Waka-Ebisu* (below). *Fugen-zō* and *Gin-Sekai* were published in 1790, *Waka-Ebisu* in 1789. Utamaro's work for the theater, the various kinds of popular novelettes, and the *kyōka-ehon* is valuable in that the works are dated and give a good idea of the chronological development of his style. Artistically speaking, the *kyōka-ehon* contain the most carefully executed work of them all. *Gin-Sekai* and *Fugen-zō*, together with another book entitled *Kyōgetsubō*, form a trilogy of *kyōka-ehon* on the theme of "snow, moon, and cherry blossom."

76. *Scene Eleven, from "Chūshingura Reenacted by Celebrated Beauties"* ◈ *ōban* ◈ published by Ōmiya ◈ Tokyo National Museum ◈ A favorite device of ukiyo-e artists was to portray beautiful women in scenes suggested (often rather remotely) by well-known episodes from history, legend, or literature. In this print, the grouping of the figures recalls a scene from *Chūshingura*, the well-known puppet drama and kabuki play based on the story of forty-seven samurai who avenge the murder of their lord, then commit suicide themselves. The writing over the figure of the young man says "Utamaro's own handsome countenance, portrayed in response to popular request."